THE
Ultimate
CHRISTIAN WEDDING
MUSIC KIT

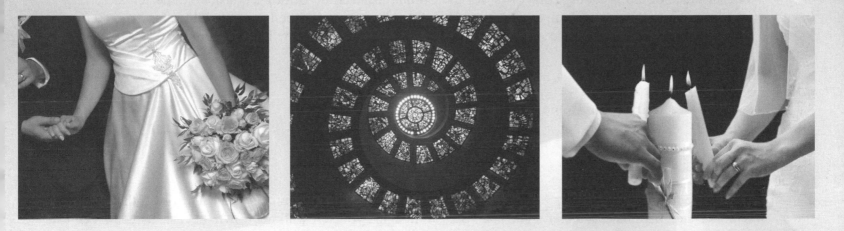

CONTEMPORARY MUSIC, PLANNING TIPS
AND MORE FOR THE PERFECT WEDDING!

Shawnee Press, Inc. &

1107 17th Avenue South • Nashville, TN 37212

Visit Shawnee Press Online at **www.shawneepress.com**

A Musical Tour of Your Wedding

The Prelude / Pre-Ceremony

This is the very beginning of the wedding, the time when the first guests arrive; sometimes refreshments and hors d'oeuvres are served before the Ceremony begins. Listen to a few songs from the included CD as you imagine the setting of your wedding and visualize your first guests arriving.

- God Causes All Things to Grow
- Household of Faith
- If You Could See What I See

The Processional

The entrance of the Wedding Party (first for the Groom, then for the Bride) is considered the actual processional. Picture your family and friends, breathlessly waiting for the Processional to start, and then your wedding party walking down the aisle as you listen to these suggested songs from the CD.

- Holding Hands
- I Will Be Here
- Love Will Be Our Home

The Bride's Entrance

This is the moment everyone's been waiting for... the moment the bride enters and walks down the aisle with her dad, parents or another significant person. Imagine yourself walking down the aisle as you listen to different choices ranging from traditional, to sweet and pretty, to upbeat and contemporary.

- Bridal Chorus *(Wagner)*
- How Beautiful
- 'Til the End of Time

The Recessional

The joyous, post-Ceremony return down the aisle of you, your spouse, and your newly joined families is the conclusion of the ceremony and is directly followed by the guests' exit. Your music can be contemporary, romantic, or traditional and joyous. Here are a few varied options:

- I Could Sing of Your Love Forever
- Morning Has Broken
- The Wedding March *(Mendelssohn)*

OPTIONS: The musical selections from various categories can be somewhat interchangeable depending on personal tastes and individual needs. You may choose to use tracks with or without a singer, or live keyboard with or without a singer.

For in depth wedding music planning, CDs and exclusive downloads visit:
www.weddingmusiccentral.com

Other Special Moments

Communion

- How Beautiful
- In Remembrance of Me
- The King of Love My Shepherd Is

The Unity Candle

An optional but increasingly popular part of the Ceremony, the unity candle is a formal candle-lighting and brief period of prayer and reflection as you join your two lives (and your families) as one.

- Close to Thee
- Parent's Prayer (Let Go of Two)
- This Flame

The Interlude / Postlude

This is the time immediately after the wedding Ceremony and just before the main Reception. It's often the time set aside for you to be congratulated formally in a receiving line, or informally while pre-dinner beverages and hors d'oeuvres are being served. Sometimes it's used for taking photos, especially when the bride and groom haven't seen each other before the ceremony out of custom or for religious reasons.

- Amazing Grace
- I Could Sing of Your Love Forever
- Love Will Be Our Home

The Reception

The time after the Ceremony is for celebrating—whether sit-down dinner, buffet or light refreshments-and it's always after the Interlude. (Not all weddings have interludes, or full dinner or dance receptions, but virtually all weddings have music.)

Most receptions start with a 'GRAND ENTRANCE' of the Bride and Groom usually accompanied by an up-beat piece of music. Sometimes, the whole wedding party is included. But this 'scene' of the wedding is usually one that's more important to brides and grooms.

- Love Will Be Our Home
- Morning Has Broken
- 'Til the End of Time

First Dance / Father-Daughter Dance

Every family has its own history and that can be reflected in the songs you choose for your dances. One of the best-loved traditions is the Father/Daughter dance. As you listen to songs on the CD, think of the different feelings you or your Dad (or new husband) may want to express.

- Butterfly Kisses
- By Heart, By Soul
- Go There With You
- We Will Dance

Contents

'Til the End of Time

Words and Music by
STEVE GREEN

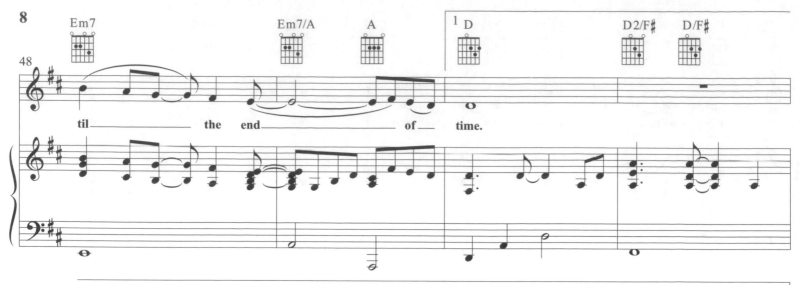

til _____ the end _____ of ____ time.

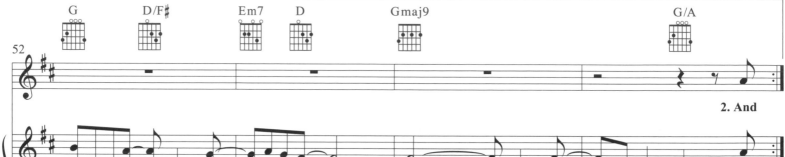

2. And

time.   And

through the ____ chang - es ____ life re - ar - rang - es, ____

I will—— have you,—— and I,—— I will hold—— you——

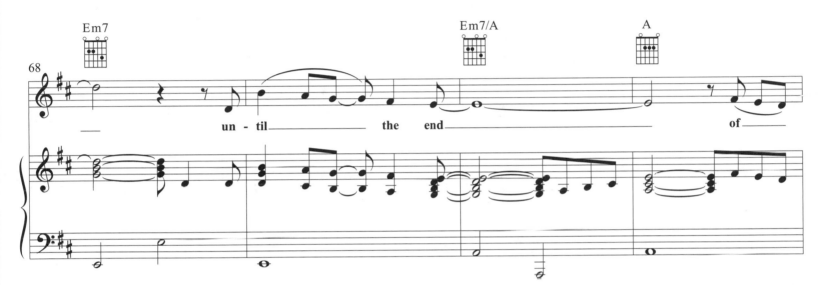

—— un - til—— the end—————————— of——

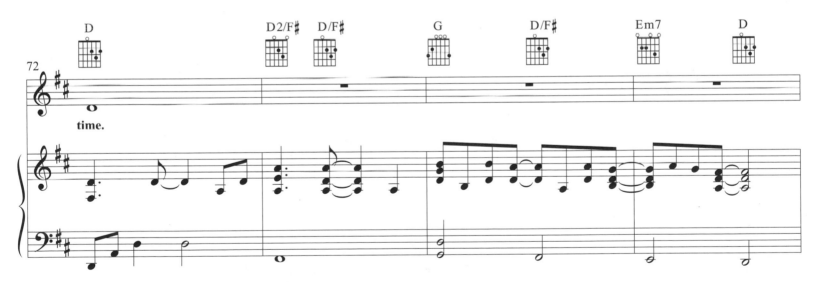

time.

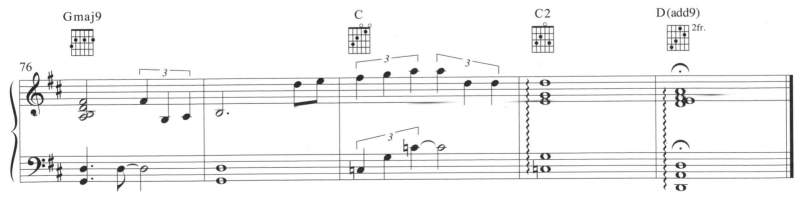

Love Will Be Our Home

Words and Music by
STEVEN CURTIS CHAPMAN

Slow two ♩ = 60

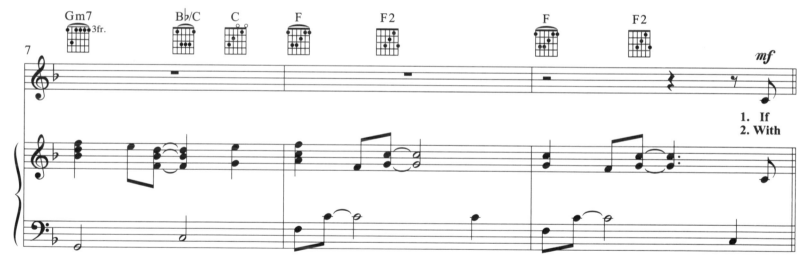

1. If home is real - ly where the heart is,
2. With love our hearts can be a fam - 'ly,

Love_____ will,   love will be_____ our home._____

_____

Love_____ will,   love will be_____ our

home._____   home._____   Wher-

ev - er there___ is laugh - ter ring - ing,   some - one smil - ing,

there are words___ of kind - ness spok - en,   where a vow is

ev - er there___ is laugh - ter ring - ing,___ some - one smil - ing,

some - one dream - ing, we can live to - geth - er there.___

'cause love will be

our home.___

I Could Sing of Your Love Forever

Words and Music by
MARTIN SMITH

O - ver the moun - tains and the sea___ Your riv - er runs___ with love for me,___

___ and I will o - pen up___ my heart and let the Heal - er set me free.___

I'm hap-py to——— be in the truth,——— and I will dai-ly lift my hands———

—— for I will al-ways sing of when Your love came down.———

I could sing of Your love——— for - ev - er.———

18

How Beautiful

Words and Music by
TWILA PARIS

Slowly ♩ = 108

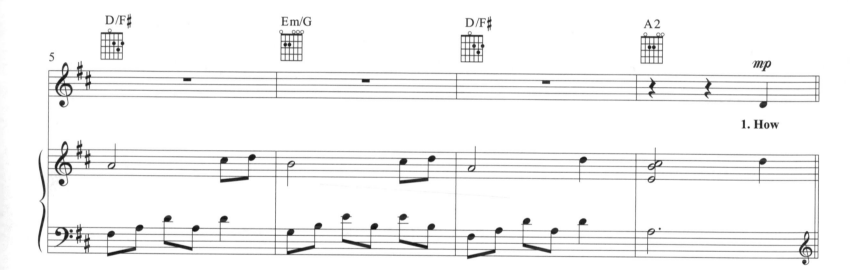

1. How

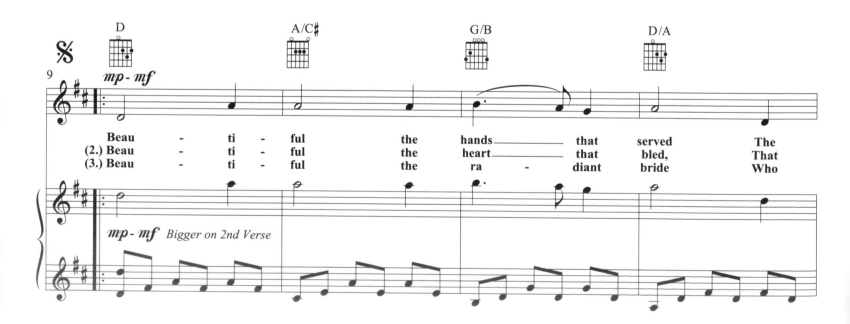

	Beau	-	ti	-	ful	the	hands	that	served	The
(2.)	Beau	-	ti	-	ful	the	heart	that	bled,	That
(3.)	Beau	-	ti	-	ful	the	ra - diant		bride	Who

mp - mf Bigger on 2nd Verse

D.S. al Coda 𝄋

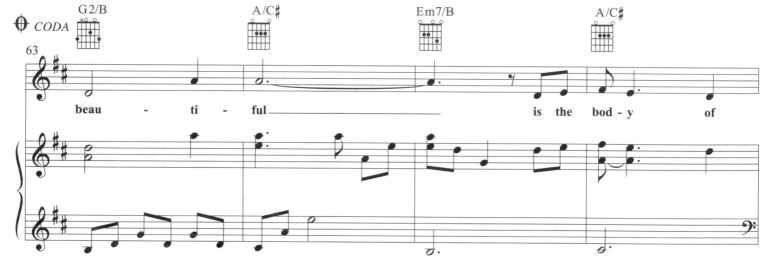

Verse 4

How beautiful the feet that bring
The sound of good news and the love of the King.
How Beautiful the hands that serve
The wine and the bread and the sons of the Earth.

By Heart, By Soul

Words and Music by
PHIL SILLAS *and* **STEPHANIE LEWIS**

Moderately slow, with a groove ♩ = 68

1. If You were a road, ___ I'd
(2.) You were a place, ___ I'd

learn ev-'ry turn ___ 'til ___ I ___ could find my way with my eyes closed. ___ If
stay my whole life ___ so ___ I ___ had ev-'ry cor-ner mem-o-rized. ___ And if

You were a song, ___ ___ I'd sing a-long ___ 'til ___ I ___ knew ev-'ry word and
You were a star, ___ I'd fol-low You home. You ___ would be ___ the Light that is my

Go There With You

Words and Music by
Steven Curtis Chapman

give my - self to love the way Love gave it - self for me, And

climb with you to moun - tain - tops or swim a rag - ing sea,_____ To the_____

place where one heart is made from two,_____ I will

go there with you._____ Oh_____ 2. I

D.S. al Coda 𝄋

take a heart whose na - ture is to beat for me___ a - lone, And

fill it up with you make all your joy and pain my own.___ No mat-ter how___

___ deep a val - ley you go through,___ I will go___

___ there with you. Whoa,___ I___ will

give my-self to love___ the way Love gave___ it-self for me,___ And

climb with you to moun-tain-tops or swim a rag-ing sea, To the

place where one heart is made from two,___ I___ will

go there with you.___ Oh,___ I will

Butterfly Kisses

Words and Music by
BOB CARLISLE *and* **RANDY THOMAS**

Bb/D   C/E   F   Gsus   G   *Last time to* ⊕

all that I've—— done wrong,—— I must have done some-thing right———— to de-serve a (her)

Bb   Bb/C   F/C   C7   Fsus   F   Fsus²⁴   F

1. (Audio Track skips the 1st ending)

hug ev-'ry morn - ing and but-ter-fly—— kiss - es at night.

Fsus   F   Fsus²⁴   F

2.

night.   All the pre-cious

Ab   Gm   Fsus²⁴   F   Bb/F   F2   F

time.———————— Oh, like the wind, the years—— go by. Pre-cious but-ter-

Household of Faith

Words by
BRENT LAMB

Music by
JOHN ROSASCO

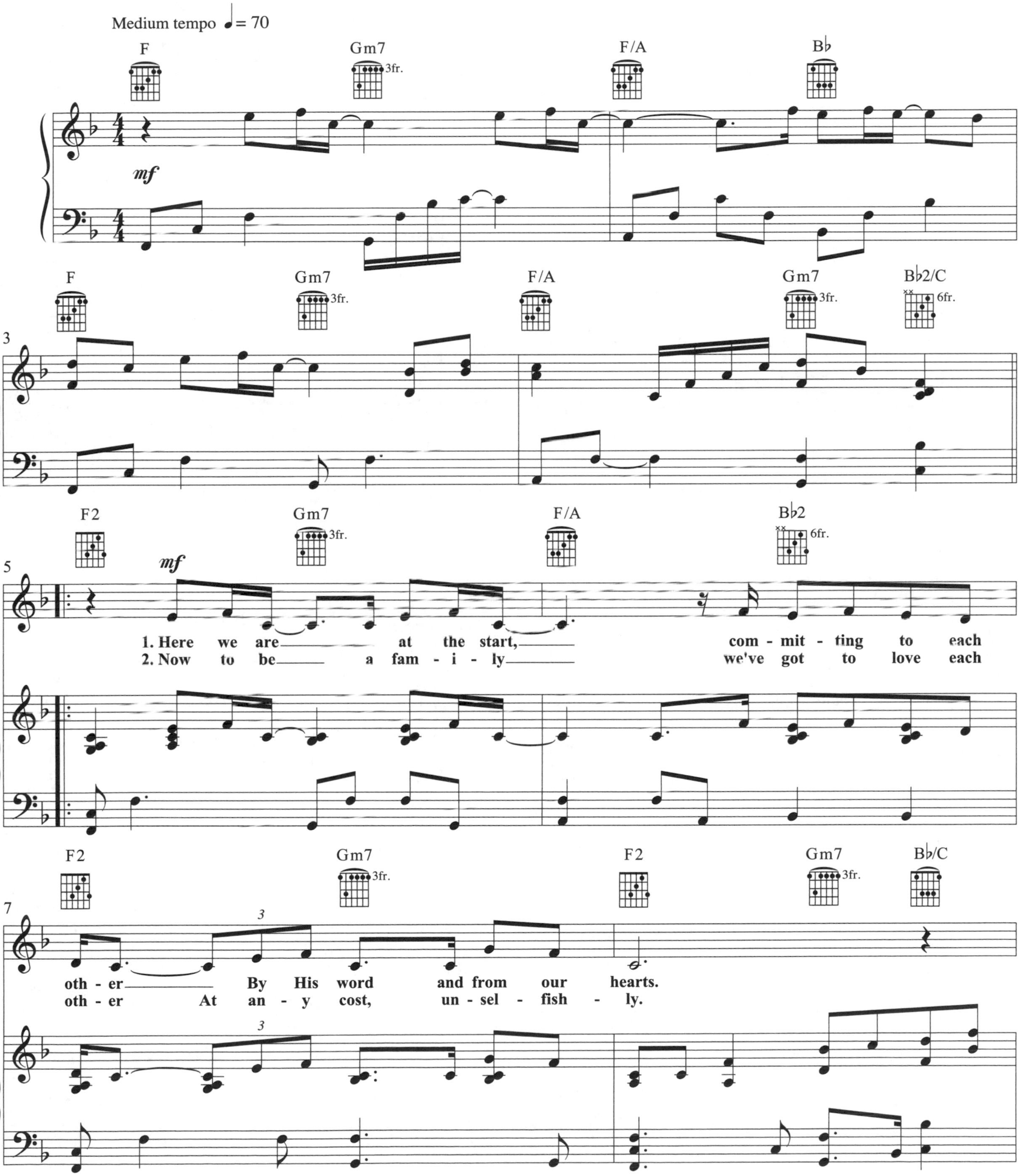

Medium tempo ♩= 70
F
Gm7
3fr.
F/A
B♭
mf
F
Gm7
3fr.
F/A
Gm7
3fr.
B♭2/C
6fr.
F2
Gm7
3fr.
F/A
B♭2
6fr.
mf
1. Here we are at the start, com - mit - ting to each
2. Now to be a fam - i - ly we've got to love each
F2
Gm7
3fr.
F2
Gm7
3fr.
B♭/C
oth - er By His word and from our hearts.
oth - er At an - y cost, un - sel - fish - ly.

God Causes All Things to Grow

Words and Music by
STEVEN CURTIS CHAPMAN
and **STEVE GREEN**

48

God caus - es all___ things to grow.___ Thru ev - 'ry sea - son, we know___

___ He will guard___ the___ life___ that He's

plant - ed in___ our souls.___ And when we feel the cold___ winds

Last time to Coda ⊕

blow, we'll hold to what___ we know: God caus - es

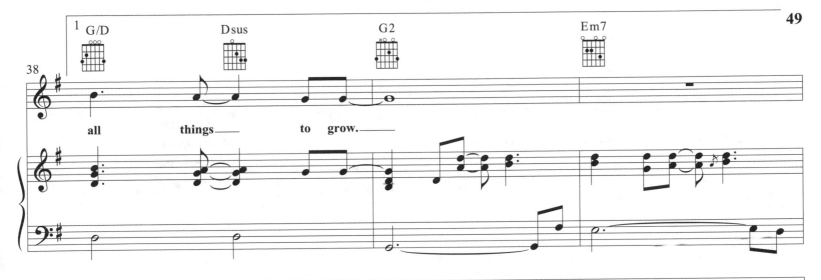

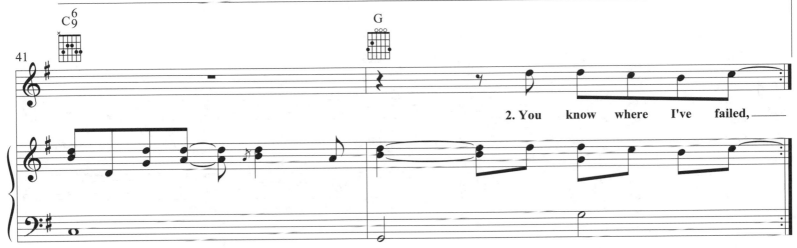

all things—— to grow.—— And we know——

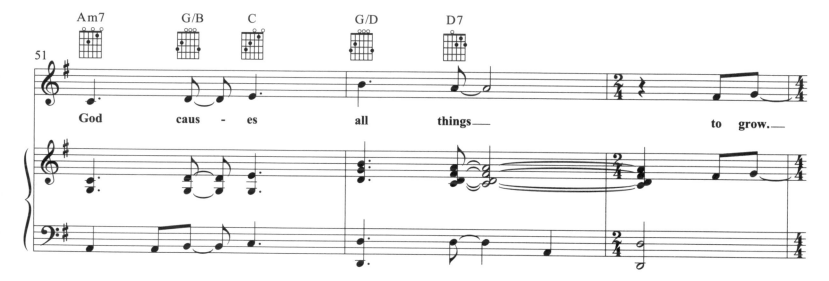

God caus - es all things—— to grow.——

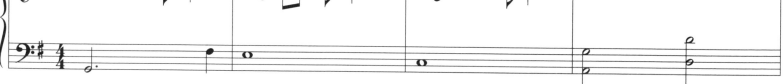

This Flame

Words and Music by
MARGARET BECKER,
RICK ELIAS *and* **LINDA ELIAS**

56

Parent's Prayer
(Let Go of Two)

Words and Music by
GREG DAVIS

1. I guess we have al - ways known — that a day — like this — one would come. —
2. Now in Your ten - der care — Lord, be all that we — can - not be. —

When our chil - dren would leave — us — and be -
And — help us to trust — You when we don't

We Will Dance

Words and Music by
STEVEN CURTIS CHAPMAN

I Will Be Here

Words and Music by
STEVEN CURTIS CHAPMAN

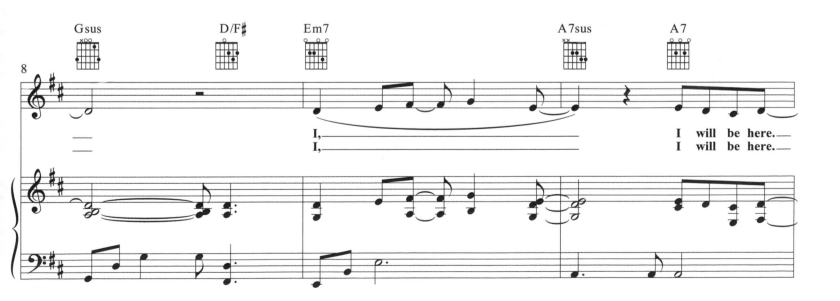

1. To-mor-row morn-ing, if you____ wake up and the sun does not____ ap-pear,
2. To-mor-row morn-ing, if you____ wake up and the fu-ture is____ un-clear,

I,_____ I will be here.____
I,_____ I will be here.____

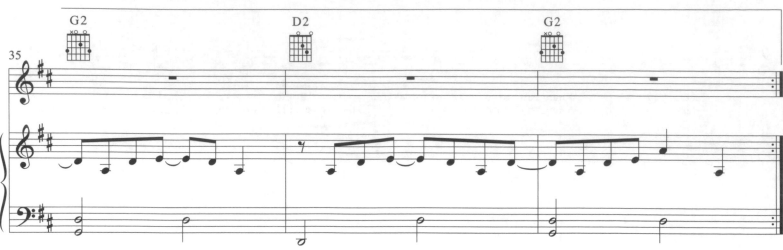

Hmm,_____ I will__ be__ true to the prom-

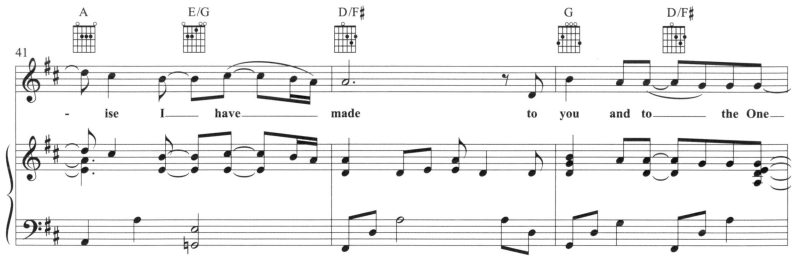

-ise I__ have_____ made to you and to____ the One__

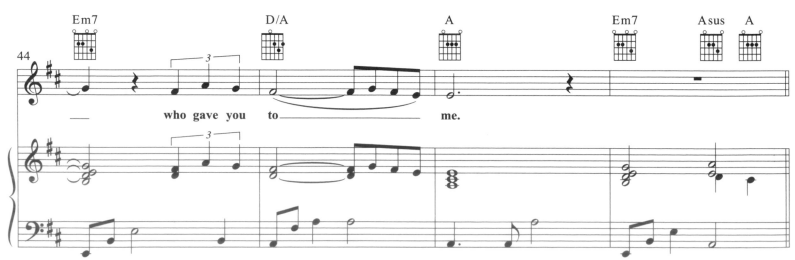

____ who gave you to_____ me.

Holding Hands

Words and Music by
STEVE GREEN, GRANT CUNNINGHAM
and **MATT HUESMANN**

Lyrics:
There's a truth we know;—
God is hold-ing us— In His
arms.—

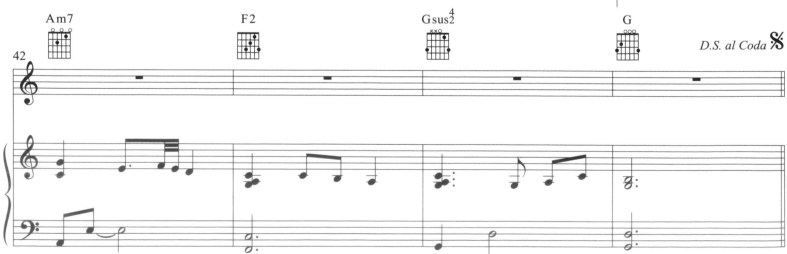

D.S. al Coda 𝄋

If You Could See What I See

Words and Music by
GEOFF MOORE and
STEVEN CURTIS CHAPMAN

In Remembrance of Me

Words and Music by
CHERI KEAGGY

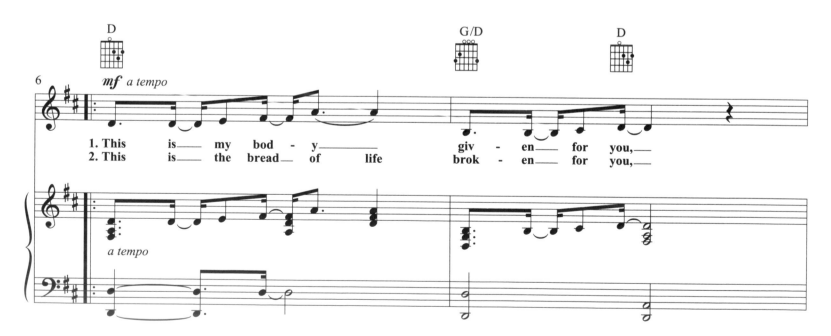

1. This is—— my bod - y—— giv - en—— for you,——
2. This is—— the bread—— of life brok - en—— for you,——

84

I will re - mem - ber the cross that You bore for me.

I will re - mem - ber the crown that You wore for me.

I will re - mem - ber the rea - son You suf - fered and

died.

3. This is my bod - y

giv - en for you,

This is the cup that holds the blood of the new cov - e - nant.

Amazing Grace

John Newton; John P. Rees, stanza 5

Traditional American melody from
Carrell and Clayton's *Virginia Harmony*, 1831

Verse 3

The Lord has promised good to me,
His word my hope secures;
He will my shield and portion be
As long as life endures.

Verse 4

Thro' many dangers, toils, and snares
I have already come.
'Tis grace hath brought me safe thus far,
And grace will lead me home.

Verse 5

When we've been there ten thousand years,
Bright shining as the sun,
We've no less days to sing God's praise
Than when we'd first begun.

Morning Has Broken

Words by
Eleanor Farjeon

Traditional Gaelic melody

Close to Thee

Fanny J. Crosby

Silas J. Vail

The King of Love My Shepherd Is

Henry W. Baker

St. Columbia
Traditional Irish melody

Where streams of living water flow,
My ransomed soul He leadeth
And, where the verdant pastures grow,
With food celestial feedeth.

Perverse and foolish oft I strayed,
But yet in love He sought me,
And on His shoulder gentle laid,
And home, rejoicing, brought me.

In death's dark vale I fear no ill,
With Thee, dear Lord, beside me,
Thy rod and staff my comfort still;
Thy cross before to guide me.

Thou spreadst a table in my sight;
Thine unction grace bestoweth;
And, oh, what transport of delight
From Thy pure chalice floweth!

Bridal March

Composed by Richard Wagner

Con moto moderato

Wedding March
(from 'A Midsummer Night's Dream')

Composed by Felix Mendelssohn

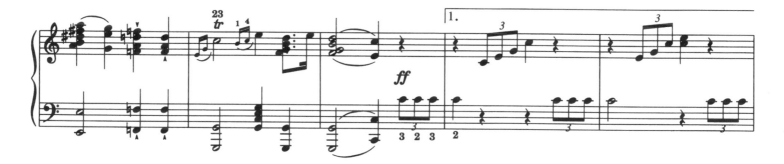

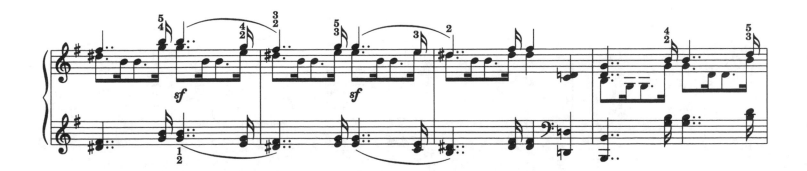

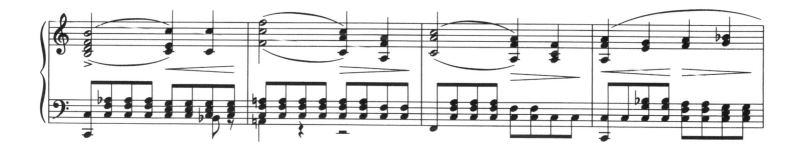

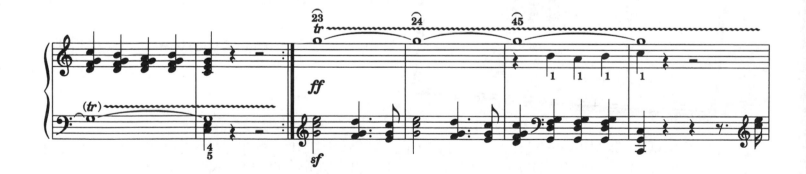

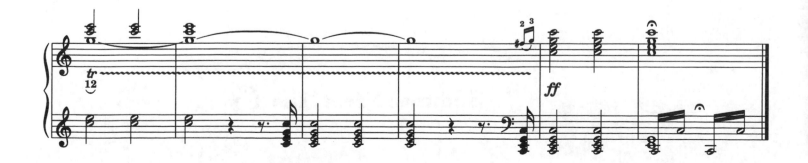

BEST-SELLING WEDDING RESOURCE!

THE ULTIMATE
WEDDING MUSIC KIT

Other than the bride and groom, music is one of most important aspects of any wedding. Make the music at your wedding something you'll cherish for a lifetime! From preludes to processionals to candle-lighting music and more, it's all here. There are also 2 CDs included containing demonstration performances of each song so you can hear the music in advance for careful preparation. The CDs also include accompaniment tracks for rehearsal or use in the wedding. In addition, there are tips on selecting music for your wedding, hiring musicians, "staging" your wedding music and more!

INCLUDES: AIR ON THE G STRING ✦ I LOVE YOU TRULY ✦ BECAUSE ✦ BRIDAL MARCH
BE THOU MY VISION ✦ FÜR ELISE ✦ TRUMPET VOLUNTARY AND SO MUCH MORE.

SB1050   PIANO/VOCAL/GUITAR COLLECTION (with 2 CDs) $29.95

Available from your favorite music supplier.
Prices and availability subject to change.

Shawnee Press, Inc. ℰ